T0158995

Could You Write a Book Comparable to

THE BOOK OF MORMON?

Could You Write a Book Comparable to

THE BOOK OF MORMON?

A List of Requirements That Must Be Met

CORY BAKER

iUniverse®

COULD YOU WRITE A BOOK COMPARABLE TO THE BOOK OF MORMON?
A LIST OF REQUIREMENTS THAT MUST BE MET

iUniverse books may be ordered through booksellers or by contacting:

iUniverse
1663 Liberty Drive
Bloomington, IN 47403
www.iuniverse.com
1-800-Authors (1-800-288-4677)

ISBN: 978-1-5320-6404-3 (sc)
ISBN: 978-1-5320-6405-0 (e)

Library of Congress Control Number: 2018914459

Print information available on the last page.

iUniverse rev. date: 01/08/2019

This book is dedicated to my family and future posterity. I want them to know that I have a testimony of the truthfulness of the Book of Mormon. This book is written out of the love and appreciation I have for it. The information herein is only supplemental to the spiritual witness I have already received of the Book of Mormon. It would bring me great joy for them to discover for themselves the truthfulness of this sacred book of scripture.

Preface

Brigham Young University professor Hugh Nibley used to challenge his students at the beginning of their semester to write a 600-page book, comparable to the Book of Mormon, and hand it in by the end of the semester. He believed this was a fair request, since the Book of Mormon was essentially written in just under three months by a 23-year-old farm boy with only a few years of education. The duration of a semester was just over three months and the college students attending his class were well educated. Many, if not all, had graduated high school, and most of the students were in their late teens or early twenties. The students should have had a clear advantage. However, none ever completed the task. It is Hugh Nibley's challenge to his students that has intrigued me to research and write about this very subject. Several of the ideas contained in this book may be attributed to the research Hugh Nibley and his contemporaries have done over the years regarding the Book of Mormon and its coming forth.

The Book of Mormon is the keystone of the Church of Jesus Christ of Latter-day Saints. It is central to the doctrines taught by the Church's members and it stands as a witness to the authenticity of the prophetic mission of Joseph Smith. If the Book of Mormon is true, then Joseph Smith was a true prophet, chosen by God to restore and organize His church on the earth. Simply put, if the Book of Mormon is what Joseph and other personal witnesses have said it is, then it is of God and therefore the Church of Jesus Christ of Latter-day Saints is God's true church on the earth and He is at the helm.

The Book of Mormon is either the greatest fictional work ever produced by man, or it is the word of God and should be considered holy scripture. Unfortunately, it doesn't typically receive the credit for either. Many are quick to judge the book as a fraud and its translator, Joseph Smith, as a deceiver. However, when examining the circumstances the book was written under, as well as looking thoroughly at the details of the contents within its pages, the truth about this marvelous work begins to unfold.

This book will put you in Joseph Smith's shoes and allow you to determine whether or not writing a comparable book is feasible under similar conditions. It may be easy to overlook the importance of the environment and the time in which the Book of Mormon was written, but in order to better understand the marvel that the Book of Mormon is, it is critical to attempt to write your book under circumstances similar to the ones Joseph Smith faced. The task to complete all the requirements listed in this book is only applicable if we assume the Book of Mormon was invented, not translated from an ancient record. As you read through this book, consider how difficult it would be for you to comply with each requirement. Any given point may be feasible if executed independently, but completing all the requirements is the only way to determine if you could, in fact, write a book comparable to the Book of Mormon.

This book is not intended to include all possible conditions, explanations, evidences, or reference materials. As modern technology progresses, and as people continue to thoroughly study the Book of Mormon, more truths will be discovered that substantiate what Joseph said about its origins. Some points in this book contain less information and fewer references than others. This is simply to allow the reader to research these points in more detail, not because more information wasn't available. This book also lists requirements that tie very closely to one particular group of people, the Hebrews. That is because the Book of Mormon was written by those of Hebrew descent. Therefore, the specific requirements that relate to the Hebrews (usually identified as Hebraisms) must be replaced by a similar writing style that pertains to the culture you choose to write about and must be of equal complexity and frequency.

Writing a book comparable to the Book of Mormon would be a tall task even for the brightest minds in our day who have the advantages of modern technology, education, peer support, and reference materials, as well as a plethora of information available at their fingertips with the assistance of the internet. By reading this book, perhaps the truth regarding the translator of the Book of Mormon and the truth of the book itself will be made apparent to you. Could anyone have written the Book of Mormon without help from God?

Requirements That Must Be Met Prior To Writing Your Book

1. You must be twenty-three years of age or younger.

Joseph Smith was born on December 23, 1805. He commenced translation of the Book of Mormon at age twenty-three in the spring of 1829. Time and experience are valuable teaching tools. Joseph, at this young age, didn't have much of either.

2. You cannot have any more than three years of formal schooling prior to writing your book.

You may be homeschooled by your parents on occasion, but your parents have limited time and resources to teach you. Joseph Smith was taught at the school of Dewey Hill by Jonathan Kinney when he and his family moved to Royalton Township. Deacon Jonathan Kinney often said, "I taught Joseph Smith, the Mormon prophet, his letters while teaching school upon Dewey Hill about the year 1810–15" (Skinner, 1906). It is estimated that he only received three years of formal schooling within that time frame. The rest of his education came at home as he describes, "I was merely instructed in reading, writing, and the ground rules of arithmetic" (Smith & Jessee, The Personal Writings of Joseph Smith, 2002). The Prophet Joseph himself was clearly unschooled in things ancient. For example, early in the work he came across words concerning a wall around Jerusalem and asked his wife, Emma, if the city indeed had walls. She affirmed what Joseph simply hadn't known (Briggs, 1884). David Whitmer described Joseph as a "man of limited education," and "ignorant of the Bible" (Cook, David Whitmer Interviews, 1991).

3. You must not be able to read or write a coherent letter.

Joseph's mother remembered that he was "less inclined to the perusal of books than any of the rest of our children" and said that at "eighteen years of age" he had "never read the Bible through in his life" (Smith L. M., 2017). Even after the Book of Mormon was produced in 1830, Joseph still struggled to spell words correctly. He wrote in his own hand in 1832 that he was "deprived of the bennifit [sic] of an education suffice it to say I was mearly [sic] instructtid [sic] in reading writing and the ground rules of Arithmatic [sic] which constituted my whole literary acquirements" (Letterbook 1, p. 1, 2017).

4. You cannot use any form of modern technology.

The internet, computers, electronic encyclopedias, and other types of smart devices were not available in the early 1800's. In order for you to write a book comparable to the Book of Mormon, you must write it under the same conditions. Therefore, you cannot use any form of technology that wasn't available in 1829.

5. You cannot use any sources for reference material.

None of the twelve people who either participated in or observed the translation mentioned Joseph having any reference materials present. (The twelve people were Emma Smith, Martin Harris, Oliver Cowdery, Elizabeth Ann Cowdery, David Whitmer, William Smith, Lucy Mack Smith, Michael Morse, Sarah Hellor Conrad, Isaac Hale, Reuben Hale, and Joseph Knight Sr.) Since the Prophet dictated openly, these individuals would have been aware of any suspicious behavior or procedures. Emma was emphatic on this very point: "He had neither manuscript nor book to read from, [and] if he had anything of the kind he could not have concealed it from me" (Cook, David Whitmer Interviews: A Restoration Witness, 1991). I say this because although David Whitmer mentions a blanket being used, it was only to partition off the living area in order to keep both the translator and scribe from the eyes of visitors (Cook, David Whitmer Interviews: A Restoration Witness, 1991). In fact, Elizabeth Anne Cowdery, Oliver's wife, said, "Joseph never had a curtain drawn between him and his scribe" (Welch & Rathbone, The Translation of the Book of Mormon: Basic Historical Information, 1986). Emma likewise said of her days as scribe, early on, that Joseph dictated "hour after hour with nothing between us" (Smith J. I., 1879). It would have been easily noticed by each scribe of the Book of Mormon if Joseph were using reference materials.

6. The places you describe in your book must be entirely unfamiliar to you. You must not have ever traveled to or seen the locations you will write about.

Joseph Smith had never traveled outside the United States prior to his work on the Book of Mormon. He was unfamiliar with the Middle East, or Near East as it is more widely known. He had never seen the landscapes or ancient civilizations of Central or South America pre-1830. In fact, the idea of cement buildings was considered preposterous in the early 1800's and many people mocked Joseph because the Book of Mormon mentions the usage of cement. Helaman 3:7, in the Book of Mormon states: "And there being but little timber upon the face of the land, nevertheless the people who went forth became exceedingly expert in the working of cement; therefore they did build houses of cement, in the which they did dwell." In 1841, when John Lloyd Stephens published his book titled "Incidents of Travel in Central America Chiapas and Yucatan", Joseph made correlations to Stephens' findings and the events of the Book of Mormon, but at the time the Book of Mormon was published he knew little to nothing about the ancient inhabitants of America.

7. The descriptions of the cultures and civilizations you provide must not be known at the time you write your book.

There are some rumors that young Joseph Smith had access to many libraries and book stores that could have provided him with materials and ideas for drafting the Book of Mormon. This concept that Joseph was a scholar and an intellectual who frequently sought out history books from the local bookstore or library is simply not true. (Refer to previous comments about Joseph being less inclined to the perusal of books than his siblings, as stated by Lucy Mack, his mother.) He had a very limited education, lived in a very isolated location, and did not have access to the major communications channels of his day, and even if he had, hardly any books were written in 1829 that discuss in detail the cultures and civilizations of the ancient Americans.

8. This must be the first book you author and publish.

One reason that Joseph's accomplishment of producing the Book of Mormon was so astonishing is that it came at the beginning of his development as a writer (supposing that he in-fact wrote or invented the book rather than translating it). It did not occur at the end of a prosperous writing career, after years of practice and experience, but came at the start of his journey. Consider the cases of Emerson, Thoreau, Hawthorne, Melville, and Whitman, and other popular writers of his time. For each of these authors there is evidence of exceptional educational opportunities or an extensive period of development as a writer, and in most circumstances both. Prior to the Book of Mormon being published in 1830, we have practically no writings from Joseph to suggest that he was capable of authoring any type of book, let alone one as substantial as the Book of Mormon.

9. The book you write will be written entirely by hand.

A quill and ink were likely used to write the Book of Mormon. "The quill pen was the primary writing instrument of the western world from the dark ages until the second third of the nineteenth century." (Daniels, 1980)

10. The book you write will be void of punctuation.

Plan to not have any punctuation in your first edition. The printer's manuscript of the Book of Mormon still exists today and demonstrates that Oliver Cowdery did not punctuate anything Joseph dictated during the translation process, likely due to the speed at which the translation took place. The chief compositor, John H. Gilbert, found that the manuscript was "closely written and legible, but not a punctuation mark from beginning to end" (Vogel, 2004); Gilbert said that he added punctuation and capitalization while working on the book in the evenings. Your book must be void of punctuation yet flow and transition smoothly from sentence to sentence, paragraph to paragraph, and chapter to chapter. Punctuation may only be added in later revisions.

11. You must invent a story about a portion of your original manuscript becoming lost, yet evidence of its existence will still be traceable in the book you write.

Joseph Smith borrowed the first 116 pages of his translation of the Book of Mormon to Martin Harris. Martin lost the manuscript of the 116 pages which purportedly contained the writings of Lehi, the father of Nephi (the current author of the first two books in the Book of Mormon). Themes and even direct statements can be found throughout the Book of Mormon that tie back to Lehi's original text, though it's not contained in the book as a separate volume. Examples are Alma 10:2,

Alma 37:38-42, Alma 50:19-20. These scriptures lend credibility to Joseph's story about the lost manuscript.

12. You must write your book from start to finish within 85 days.

The entire Book of Mormon, save a few pages—with Joseph's wife, Emma, acting as scribe prior to April 7—was translated and written between April 7 and June 30, 1829. After reviewing all the other conditions and circumstances in this book, it will become evident that Joseph Smith actually only had about 57 days during which he and his scribes could have translated. That works out to be an average of eight pages per day. Either way, the translation moved at a very rapid pace. In a lecture given by BYU professor John Welch he stated,

> In stabilizing historical judgments, one always looks for certain anchor points that hold in place the structural girders of our historical understanding. ... I propose that these five anchor dates in particular can be tied down with near-historical-certainty. They are based on credible, contemporaneous, primary sources, found in independent documents. They show that, with the possible exception of a page or two, the entire Book of Mormon came forth, day after day, and hour by

> hour, between April 7 and June 30. (Toone, 2017)

Welch's five anchor dates:

- April 7, with Cowdery acting as scribe in Harmony, Pennsylvania.
- May 15, as documented by testimonies given by Cowdery and Lucy Mack Smith, Joseph's mother.
- May 31, when the Title Page of the Book of Mormon was translated.
- June 11, when Joseph Smith obtained the copyright from the Library of Congress.
- June 30, the established date for completion of the translation. Cowdery began to copy the Printer's Manuscript in July so it could go to press.

With that timeframe established, Welch counted the number of days between April 7 and June 30, which is eighty-five. Subtracting eleven full days for trips or times when Joseph was identifiably occupied, leaves seventy-four days. Subtract another sixteen days of about half-time distractions or other interruptions (business, farming, chores, personal time, visitors, Sundays, church matters and other distractions), and it's down to fifty-eight. Another day is taken away for work to receive thirteen revelations and you are left with fifty-seven.

Requirements That Must Be Met While Writing Your Book

13. You must work on other publications simultaneously.

Joseph dictated to Oliver Cowdery, word-by-word, revelations he received for at least thirteen sections of Doctrine and Covenants during the period in which he also translated the Book of Mormon. (Sections 6-18) The total word count of these sections is 7,173. These revelations included instructions for building the church, calling the twelve apostles, personal revelations for those who would become witnesses of the Book of Mormon, as well as a revelation for Joseph Knight, information about John, the beloved disciple, the restoration of the Aaronic Priesthood, what happened to the 116 lost pages, the evil designs of those who would try to destroy this work, and more.

14. You must fulfill family responsibilities.

Joseph still had to perform his duties as a husband and provider while translating the Book of Mormon. He most assuredly helped with the duties around the house and reserved time to be with his wife, family and close friends even during the arduous translation process.

15. You must move your family and all your belongings during the middle of your work.

Joseph and his family relocated from Harmony to Fayette to live with the Whitmers during the end of May and early June 1829. This undoubtedly interrupted the work on the translation of the Book of Mormon. An interruption such as this, while in the middle of writing your book, is important to consider because you must account not only for the lack of time Joseph had, but also the distractions he faced during the 85-day translation period. This distraction would have made it more difficult to originate the complex stories, characters, and plots currently found within the Book of Mormon.

16. When you start writing your book, you must begin at the middle of the story, work till the end of the story, then go back and write the beginning.

Joseph began his translation with the book of Mosiah, which begins on page 153 in the first edition of the Book of Mormon. Joseph translated from Mosiah through

Moroni and then translated from 1 Nephi through the Words of Mormon. In the middle of translating those books, he also worked on the translation of the Title Page, which had to have been completed by June 11, when it was used as part of the copyright application process.

17. After pauses for sleep, food, or other activities, you must never review the last sentence or paragraph you wrote. You must start right where you stopped previously.

Emma Smith said of the inspired process: "After meals, or after interruptions, [Joseph] would at once begin where he had left off, without either seeing the manuscript or having any portion of it read to him" (Smith J. I., 1879). Alma 36 quotes Lehi's vision, word for word, in 1 Nephi 1:8, 319 pages earlier in the first edition. If Joseph never asked to be read back any previous sections he had dictated, how did he quote the exact words of Lehi? In 1 Nephi 19:11-12 Nephi recorded the prophecy of Zenos concerning the destruction that would come upon the wicked. Zenos listed ten specific calamities including lightning, fire, vapor of darkness, and more. These same ten calamities are shown to have occurred prior to Christ's visit to the Americas in 3 Nephi 8:6-23, 420 pages later in the first edition. In Mosiah 2:13, King Benjamin listed five legal prohibitions: murder, plunder, theft, adultery and any manner of wickedness. These same exact five prohibitions are found seven other times throughout the Book of Mormon as part of Nephite formulated law.

Requirements That Your Book Must Contain

18. Your book must have a minimum of 588 pages with approximately 450 words per page.

The first edition of the Book of Mormon was 588 pages. Computerized word counts vary of the original 1830 edition. They range from about 267,000 to 270,745 words. Thus, each original page of the 1830 edition had an average of about 450 words per page.

19. Your book must contain the equivalent of 239 chapters: 54 about war, 21 about history, 55 about prophecy, 71 about doctrine, 17 about missionaries, and 21 about the mission of Jesus Christ.

The Book of Mormon did not contain chapters originally, and it would be even more challenging to write the equivalent of each of these groups without organizing them into chapters, and yet still be consistent.

20. You must create 337 proper names for your story; 188 unique names that can be found nowhere else. These names must be derivatives of the language(s) and culture(s) you write about.

Hundreds of individual characters and place names are presented in the Book of Mormon and can be tracked comprehensibly throughout. The names used have connections to ancient languages.

> The Book of Mormon contains 337 proper names and 21 gentilics (or analogous forms) based on proper names. . . . Of these 337 proper names, 188 are unique to the Book of Mormon, while 149 are common to the Book of Mormon and the Bible. If the textual passages common to the Book of Mormon and the Bible are excluded, 53 names occur in both books. (Ludlow, 1992)

> The proper names of the Book of Mormon can provide information about the text and the language(s) used to compose it. When studied with apposite methodology, these names testify to the ancient origin of the Book of Mormon. For example, Jershon is the toponym for a land given by the Nephites to a group of Lamanites as an inheritance. Based on the

> usual correspondence in the King James Version of j for the Hebrew phoneme /y/, the Book of Mormon Jershon could correspond to the Hebrew root yrs meaning 'to inherit,' thus providing an appropriate play on words in Alma 27:22: 'and this land Jershon is the land which we will give unto our brethren for an inheritance.' Similarly, one Book of Mormon name used for a man that might have seemed awkward, Alma, now is known from two second-century A.D. Hebrew documents of the Bar Kokhba period (Yadin, p. 176) and thus speaks for a strong and continuing Hebrew presence among Book of Mormon Peoples. (Ludlow, 1992)

There are many names in the Book of Mormon that have ties to the Egyptian and Hebrew languages. It seems unlikely that Joseph could have made up so many names that not only have connections to both languages but that fit properly into the storyline, considering he hadn't studied either language prior to 1829. Many Hebrew names found in the Book of Mormon, but not in the Bible, have been discovered in ancient Semitic texts and inscriptions (like the name Alma, mentioned previously) thus providing more evidence to suggest that the names contained therein are authentic. Only a few names included in the Book of Mormon were familiar to Joseph Smith. He was certainly acquainted with the names of Joseph, Samuel and perhaps even Benjamin, and it would seem sensible for these Hebrew names to have been included, since the Book of Mormon was written by people of Hebrew descent.

The names of Korihor, Pahoran, Paanchi, Pacumeni have ties to the ancient Egyptian names Herihor, Pahura, Piankh/Piankhy and Pamenches respectively. Amun is one of the most common root names in Egypt, and it is also a common root name in the Book of Mormon. The following names have links to Amun: Laman, Ammon, Ammonihah, Lamoni, Cumeni, Helaman, Kishkumen, Kumenonhi, and Pacumeni. We should expect the Book of Mormon to contain several Egyptian names, or names with root meanings in Egyptian, since Nephi stated at the very beginning of his account: "Yea, I make a record in the language of my father, which consists of the learning of the Jews and the language of the Egyptians." (1 Nephi 1:2, The Book of Mormon, 2013)

> Joseph Smith may not have realized that Ammon was the name of the Egyptian 'god of the empire' in Lehi's day, or he might have been more careful in using it. Other names derived from Ammon (consistent with Egyptian name-forming practices) include Aminidab, Aminadi, Amnihu, and Amnor, following an ancient linguistic procedure somehow worked out by Joseph Smith. Gadianton and

Gidianhi (a couple of robbers); Gideon, Gilead, Gilgal, Gid, Gidgiddonah, and Gidgiddoni (all military leaders or strategists). Gidgiddonah and Gidgiddoni both come from the same Egyptian stem and mean 'Thoth hath said I shall live' and 'Thoth hath said we shall live.' Gidianhi was a 'typical Egyptian name' meaning 'Thoth is my life.' Did Joseph Smith even know Thoth was considered one of the most important Egyptian gods? Gentilics (derivations of names of persons or lands), including Lamoni (which means 'Lamanite'—which he was), Muloki (which probably comes from 'Mulekite'), and Moroni (which means 'coming from the land of Moron,' a Book of Mormon land). This is only a sample. Scholars have traced these and other names largely to ancient Egyptian and Hebrew languages, 'with a sprinkling of Hittite, Arabic, and Greek.' They assert that the variations on the names follow correct rules. So these names are linguistically and culturally justifiable—confusing though they may be. Even if someone were to suggest that inventing that number of names in a severely limited time frame might have been possible, their consistency with language

> patterns yet to be discovered removes it far from the realm of probability. (Black & Wilcox, 2011)

It is interesting to ponder not only the considerable quantity of names Joseph Smith would have had to invent if he truly wrote the Book of Mormon, but also the strenuous task of connecting those names to the known civilizations and languages of both the Egyptians and Hebrews. That adds another large layer of improbability for Joseph.

21. You must invent a language for the people in your book, then produce several sample characters or letters from that language for experts to examine.

Joseph Smith provided a copy of the characters written on the golden plates to Martin Harris. This copy, which Joseph said was written in "reformed Egyptian" (the original language of the Book of Mormon) has not been recovered. However, Martin Harris brought some characters Joseph had copied from the plates to Charles Anthon, a well-known classical scholar of Columbia University, seeking an expert opinion on the authenticity of the characters and the translation. In Martin's words, he recorded, "I then showed him those which were not yet translated, and he said that they were Egyptian, Chaldaic, Assyriac, and Arabic; and he said they were true characters" (Smith J., Pearl of Great Price, Joseph Smith History, 1:64, 2013).

22. Your book must include a history of an ancient land that spans over 2,600 years.

The history of the Jaredites begins at the time of the Tower of Babel around 2,200 B.C. and their account is woven into the Nephite record upon the discovery of Coriantumr by the people of Zarahemla (Mulekites). The history of the Nephites is finalized by Moroni in the year 421 A.D.

23. Include in your story, the history of at least four individual nations.

The Book of Mormon primarily tells the history of the Lamanites and Nephites but it also includes the history of the Mulekites and Jaredites. Each of these groups traveled to America at different times. The histories of these nations are combined and inter-shuffled into one free-flowing story.

24. You must describe in detail the religious, ethnic, economic, social, cultural, and political institutions of the peoples in your book.

> The Book of Mormon contains a complex system of religious teachings. These are presented in unique ways by different prophets in their own times and contexts. Lehi reports a vision of the tree of life. Nephi presents the gospel of Jesus Christ

> in conjunction with the vision of Christ's baptism. Jacob reports Zenos's allegory of the olive tree. Benjamin gives a great temple sermon. Alma teaches that the word of God is a seed which must be planted and nourished. Jesus Christ gives the Nephites a modified version of his Sermon on the Mount. Each of these enrich understanding of the basic teachings; they never confuse them or contradict one another. (Reynolds, 1997)

The Book of Mormon describes numerous ethnic interactions without ever misplacing or losing track of even the most minor groups. They can be accurately traced throughout the entire storyline. A complex monetary system is described in detail in the eleventh chapter of the book of Alma. Further details of the economic portion are described in the fortieth point of this book. The Nephites were ruled by hereditary kings for about 500 years once they arrived in the Americas. Then around 91 B.C. the reign of the judges commenced, which lasted until Christ's personal visit to the Americas, when he established a form of church government. That continued for a couple centuries until there was an eventual breakdown of society into tribal groups, just prior to the destruction of the Nephites.

> Subtle and complex political traditions evolve early in the text and surface in a

> variety of forms in later sections, always plausibly and consistently. The complaints Laman and Lemuel raise against Nephi in their earliest murmuring evolve into a national ideology that is still being invoked 500 years later to justify Lamanite efforts to subjugate their Nephite brethren. (Reynolds, 1997)

25. You must accurately trace a timeline throughout your book.

In the Book of Mormon different events were used to reckon time from: the time Lehi left Jerusalem, the initiation of the reign of the judges, and the day the sign was given for the birth of Jesus Christ. Yet no confusion results and dating sequences can always be reconstructed precisely. These timelines also coincide with the events in the Bible. The very first chapter in the Book of Mormon links its timeline to that of the Bible's during the reign of King Zedekiah of Judah. "For it came to pass in the commencement of the first year of the reign of Zedekiah, king of Judah, (my father, Lehi, having dwelt at Jerusalem in all his days); and in that same year there came many prophets, prophesying unto the people that they must repent, or the great city Jerusalem must be destroyed" (1 Nephi 1:4). Your timeline must be consistent throughout even though you use different ways to measure the time.

26. You must include genealogies in your book that match the timeline you've provided.

The Bible contains several long genealogies, demonstrating the importance of genealogical records to the Jews. Assuming the Book of Mormon is authentic, it would make sense to include several genealogies, which in-fact it does. For example, the first chapter of Ether contains a list of thirty different kings from Ether all the way back to Jared. This list of kings serves as an outline for the entire book, but in reverse order. The story and timeline provided thereafter coincide with the genealogy provided at the beginning of the book.

27. You must include intermittent narration throughout your book.

Mormon was the original editor, compiler and abridger of nearly the entire Nephite history spanning approximately one thousand years. His comments are found scattered throughout the text of the Book of Mormon. When examined carefully, his abridgement, editing, and compilation work can also be identified. One example of the impressive work Mormon did (that Joseph would have had to orally dictate if he were indeed the author) can be found in Alma chapter 20. In this chapter there are five total voices heard, one of them is the voice of the editor and abridger Mormon. I have inserted parenthesis each time the person speaking changes.

1. (Mormon) And it came to pass that when they had established a church in that land, that king Lamoni desired that Ammon should go with him to the land of Nephi, that he might show him unto his father.
2. And the voice of the Lord came to Ammon, saying: (The Lord) Thou shalt not go up to the land of Nephi, for behold, the king will seek thy life; but thou shalt go to the land of Middoni; for behold, thy brother Aaron, and also Muloki and Ammah are in prison.
3. (Mormon) Now it came to pass that when Ammon had heard this, he said unto Lamoni: (Ammon) Behold, my brother and brethren are in prison at Middoni, and I go that I may deliver them.
4. (Mormon) Now Lamoni said unto Ammon: (King Lamoni) I know, in the strength of the Lord thou canst do all things. But behold, I will go with thee to the land of Middoni; for the king of the land of Middoni, whose name is Antiomno, is a friend unto me; therefore I go to the land of Middoni, that I may flatter the king of the land, and he will cast thy brethren out of prison. (Mormon) Now Lamoni said unto him: (King Lamoni) Who told thee that thy brethren were in prison?
5. (Mormon) And Ammon said unto him: (Ammon) No one hath told me, save it be God; and he said unto me— (The Lord) Go and deliver thy brethren, for they are in prison in the land of Middoni.

6. (Mormon) Now when Lamoni had heard this he caused that his servants should make ready his horses and his chariots.

There are a total of twelve voice changes in those verses. Four voices are distinctly marked. The Book of Mormon is filled with these types of examples and dialogues that go on for entire chapters. Like the Book of Mormon, your book must also contain this same type of complex narration throughout. Here are a few other examples of Mormon's commentaries: Helaman 3:13-17, Helaman 12, 3 Nephi 5:8-26, 3 Nephi 10:11-19, 3 Nephi 26:8-21 and the entire chapter of 4 Nephi.

28. You must include large embedded flashbacks in your story and at least one embedded flashback within a flashback.

A strong indication that the Book of Mormon is a real, historical, abridged record, rather than a story crafted by the imagination of Joseph Smith, can be found in Mormon's flashbacks in the book of Alma. Shortly after Alma and the sons of Mosiah are reunited, Mormon takes the opportunity to retell their experiences. In Alma chapters 17-27 he seamlessly integrates the details of past events, not by simply copying the previous stories word for word, but by using his own words to tell them. He adds new details that hadn't been mentioned previously. Mormon fits these stories perfectly into the narrative and the original story immediately resumes following his inserted flashbacks. Not only does the Book of Mormon contain several flashbacks, but it contains at least one flashback within a flashback (Alma 20:30–Alma 21:14). Keeping the narrative smooth and free of error during the telling of these events and then incorporating them back into the original story without distracting from the storyline would be a difficult challenge.

29. Include exact word-for-word copies of previous statements or quotes from your book. Remember, you cannot look back at the text that's already been written. You must do it by memory alone.

One example of this can be found in Helaman 14:12, which is a 21-word verbatim quote from King Benjamin's speech recorded in Mosiah 3:8. It states "Jesus Christ, the Son of God, the Father of heaven and of earth, the Creator of all things from the beginning." This specific quote is found over 200 pages after it was originally recorded in Mosiah, yet Joseph never referred back to the manuscript containing the writings he had already translated for assistance (See point 14 for details). For him to have had such a memory would be astonishing indeed.

30. Your book must contain tens of thousands of original phrases.

The Book of Mormon has often been accused of plagiarizing the Bible or other books such as the Solomon

Spaulding manuscript or the *View of the Hebrews*. Nevertheless, it contains tens of thousands of three-to-seven word phrases not found anywhere else, including those books. In Randal A. Wright's book titled *The Book of Mormon Miracle*, he estimates there to be over 45,000 original phrases in the Book of Mormon, showing that the overwhelming majority of the Book of Mormon is original.

31. You must include authentic legal cases.

Here are a few examples of legal cases in the Book of Mormon: the case of Paanchi, the case of Sherem against Jacob, the trial of Abinadi, the trial of Nehor, the trial of Seantum, the trial of Alma and Amulek, the trial of Korihor, the trial of Pachus's men and the King Men, and the execution of Zemnarihah. Each of these legal cases was handled distinctly, subject to the circumstance and type of government system at the time of the trial.

32. Weave into your book a history of Jesus Christ and his dealings with the ancient people(s) along with the pattern of Christian living.

The Nephites abided by the Law of Moses for many generations, until the resurrection and visitation of Jesus Christ to the Americas, when He taught them the principles of faith, repentance, baptism, service, temple worship etc. (though these gospel principles which also coincide with biblical teachings, are found all throughout the Book of Mormon). The Messiah is mentioned in the very first chapter of the first book of Nephi in the Book of Mormon. Prophecies of Him are scattered throughout. Refer to the following for more examples: 1 Nephi 11:33, 1 Nephi 19:8, 1 Nephi 22:12, 1 Nephi 22:21, 2 Nephi 2:8, 2 Nephi 6:17, 2 Nephi 10:3, 2 Nephi 25:13, 2 Nephi 25:19, Mosiah 3:8, Mosiah 13:33, Mosiah 15:1, Mosiah 16:15, Alma 7:10, Alma 21:9, Helaman 5:9, Helaman 8:22, Helaman 14:2, 3 Nephi 9:16, Ether 3:14.

33. You must reference Jesus Christ 3,925 times.

This is the total number of times Jesus Christ is referenced in the Book of Mormon per the research cited by Susan Ward Easton (Easton, 1978). There are 6,607 verses in the current Book of Mormon. This means that Christ is referenced on average about every 1.7 verses.

34. You must not make any contradictory statements.

The Book of Mormon is very consistent and any purported contradictions it contains have good explanations. For example, in 2 Nephi 5:14-16, some people have suggested that verses 15 and 16 contradict each other because one verse states that all manner of wood, iron, copper brass, steel and gold were in abundance, while the following verse states that so many precious things (presumably the metals aforementioned) were "…not to be found upon the land." However, we can see that in verse 15 Nephi is stating how he instructed his people to work with all types of wood, metal and precious ores. We don't know what kind of ores he's referring to other than what he specifically mentions previously. In verse 16 he speaks about the building of a temple "like unto the temple of Solomon" and that the workmanship was "exceedingly fine," even though it was "not built of so many precious things"; even though gold was in abundance maybe there wasn't as much as it would have required to make a full replica of Solomon's large temple. Possibly he was referring to gems such as rubies or sapphires that could have been in the temple. There is certainly some ambiguity here, and we are left to interpret what Nephi was saying.

Many people have pointed out that the Book of Mormon states Jesus was born at Jerusalem. Everyone knows that he was born in Bethlehem. However, Alma chapter 7:10 states: "And behold, he shall be born of Mary, at Jerusalem which is the land of our forefathers,". The term land was often used to indicate the rural area and villages associated with a larger city with the same name. Bethlehem is only five miles from Jerusalem and would certainly fall in its economic sphere as a smaller village at the time Christ was born. Furthermore, scholars have actually found ancient textual references to Bethlehem "in the land of Jerusalem."

The Journal of Book of Mormon Studies provides yet another example of a supposed contradiction:

> In the preface to the 1830 edition of the Book of Mormon, Joseph Smith wrote that the lost 116 pages included his translation of 'the Book of Lehi, which was an account abridged from the plates of Lehi, by the hand of Mormon.' However, in Doctrine and Covenants 10:44, the Lord told Joseph that the lost pages contained 'an abridgment of the account of Nephi.' (The Doctrine and Covenants of the Church of Jesus Christ of Latter-day Saints, 2013) Some critics have argued that these statements are contradictory and therefore somehow provide evidence that Joseph Smith was not a prophet. However, a more careful reading of the Book of Mormon demonstrates that this criticism is invalid. (Sloan, 1997)

There are a few possible scenarios here, but the most likely is that Nephi copied the words of his father, in the same manner that he copied sections of Isaiah from the brass plates. That way his account would contain, in a sense, the plates of Lehi or the Book of Lehi. Nephi stated, "And upon the plates which I made I did engraven the record of my father, and also our journeyings in the wilderness, and the prophecies of my father; and also many of mine own prophecies have I engraven upon them" (1 Nephi 19:1). It was also common for the plates of an author to be referred to as their own, when in fact they were written by another. Take the case of Jacob, Nephi's younger brother. Jacob's record was written by Nephi according to his own words, "These plates are called the plates of Jacob, and they were made by the hand of Nephi" (Jacob 3:14). Therefore, it would also make sense for the plates of Lehi to have been written by Nephi. Whatever the case, there is clear evidence to support that it is not a contradiction. It is entirely reasonable to expect the Book of Mormon to contain some errors, but this is not one of them. There are many more criticisms like these, but if they are examined carefully, the truth can be identified. You must take extra care to ensure your book does not contain contradictions.

35. You must include and maintain two distinct perspectives throughout your book; one from each of the two main peoples described in your book.

Throughout the Book of Mormon there are two distinct points of view. One is of the Nephites, the primary authors of the book, and the other is of the Lamanites, whose view consistently opposes the Nephites. A good example of this is found early in Nephi's record where Laman and Lemuel proclaim,

> And thou art like unto our father, led away by the foolish imaginations of his heart; yea, he hath led us out of the land of Jerusalem, and we have wandered in the wilderness for these many years; and

> our women have toiled, being big with child; and they have borne children in the wilderness and suffered all things, save it were death; and it would have been better that they had died before they came out of Jerusalem than to have suffered these afflictions. Behold, these many years we have suffered in the wilderness, which time we might have enjoyed our possessions and the land of our inheritance; yea, and we might have been happy. (1 Nephi 17:20,21)

Notice the reasoning for their anger. They blamed Nephi (their younger brother) and Lehi (their father) for their visions (which they call foolish imaginations), which essentially were the reason they left their lands, inheritance, and material possessions. They also blamed them for all their suffering in the wilderness, which was so intense they would have preferred death. This perspective is carried throughout the Book of Mormon. The Lamanites never forget their suffering, loss of their inheritance, and in Laman's case, the right to rule. Refer to Mosiah 10:12-17, Alma 20:10-13 and Alma 54:16-24 for a few examples of how this viewpoint was passed along for over 1,000 years and sprinkled throughout the text of the Book of Mormon.

36. You must interlace scriptures from the Holy Bible into your book.

Hugh Nibley wrote:

> [One of the] most devastating arguments against the Book of Mormon was that it actually quoted the Bible. The early critics were simply staggered by the incredible stupidity of including large sections of the Bible in a book which they insisted was specifically designed to fool the Bible-reading public. They screamed blasphemy and plagiarism at the top of their lungs, but today any biblical scholar knows that it would be extremely suspicious if a book purporting to be the product of a society of pious emigrants from Jerusalem in ancient times did not quote the Bible. No lengthy religious writing of the Hebrews could conceivably be genuine if it was not full of scriptural quotations. (Nibley, 1989)

The Book of Mormon quotes Isaiah chapters 2–14, 48–51, 53, 54, and most of 52. The King James Version of the Bible contains the phrase "it is written" sixty-nine times in the New Testament. The Old Testament contains this phrase another twenty-four times. Generally following that phrase is a direct quote from a previous book of scripture demonstrating that the Old Testament quotes itself and the New Testament frequently quotes the Old Testament. Close examination of the Old Testament reveals many passages which are copied nearly word for word, including grammatical errors. Micah, who lived hundreds of years after Isaiah, copies word for word in Micah 4:1-3 from Isaiah's prophecy in Isaiah 2:2-4 without once giving him credit. We also find the genealogy from Genesis 5:10-11,36 repeated in 1 Chronicles. Much of the history in Samuel and Kings is repeated in Chronicles, and Isaiah 36:2 through Isaiah 38:5 is the same as 2 Kings 18:17 through 2 Kings 20:6. Why would the authors of different books in the Bible copy previously written scriptures? Whatever the reason, the Book of Mormon follows suit, demonstrating the same patterns of biblical writers, further evidence that the book was written by Hebrews.

37. Your book must fulfill Bible prophecies.

Jesus told his apostles "And other sheep I have, which are not of this fold: them also I must bring, and they shall hear my voice; and there shall be one fold, and one shepherd" (John 10:16). This was fulfilled after Jesus' resurrection when he came to the American continent and said to the Nephites,

> And verily I say unto you, that ye are they of whom I said: Other sheep I have which are not of this fold; them also I must bring, and they shall hear my voice; and there shall be one fold, and one shepherd. And they understood me

> not, for they supposed it had been the Gentiles; for they understood not that the Gentiles should be converted through their preaching. And they understood me not that I said they shall hear my voice; and they understood me not that the Gentiles should not at any time hear my voice—that I should not manifest myself unto them save it were by the Holy Ghost. But behold, ye have both heard my voice, and seen me; and ye are my sheep, and ye are numbered among those whom the Father hath given me. (3 Nephi 15:21-24)

Psalms 85:11 states: "Truth shall spring out of the earth; and righteousness shall look down from heaven." The Book of Mormon literally sprang out of the earth. In Isaiah 29:11,12 the prophet writes "And the vision of all is become unto you as the words of a book that is sealed, which men deliver to one that is learned, saying, Read this, I pray thee: and he saith, I cannot; for it is sealed: And the book is delivered to him that is not learned, saying, Read this, I pray thee: and he saith, I am not learned." Isaiah prophesied what would happen when the Book of Mormon (or at least a portion of the book) was brought to professor Charles Anthon. Joseph recorded in Joseph Smith History 1:63-65:

> Sometime in this month of February, the aforementioned Mr. Martin Harris came

to our place, got the characters which I had drawn off the plates, and started with them to the city of New York. For what took place relative to him and the characters, I refer to his own account of the circumstances, as he related them to me after his return, which was as follows: "I went to the city of New York, and presented the characters which had been translated, with the translation thereof, to Professor Charles Anthon, a gentleman celebrated for his literary attainments. Professor Anthon stated that the translation was correct, more so than any he had before seen translated from the Egyptian. I then showed him those which were not yet translated, and he said that they were Egyptian, Chaldaic, Assyriac, and Arabic; and he said they were true characters. He gave me a certificate, certifying to the people of Palmyra that they were true characters, and that the translation of such of them as had been translated was also correct. I took the certificate and put it into my pocket, and was just leaving the house, when Mr. Anthon called me back, and asked me how the young man found out that there were gold plates in the place where he found them. I answered that an angel of

> God had revealed it unto him. "He then said to me, 'Let me see that certificate.' I accordingly took it out of my pocket and gave it to him, when he took it and tore it to pieces, saying that there was no such thing now as ministering of angels, and that if I would bring the plates to him he would translate them. I informed him that part of the plates were sealed, and that I was forbidden to bring them. He replied, 'I cannot read a sealed book.' I left him and went to Dr. Mitchell, who sanctioned what Professor Anthon had said respecting both the characters and the translation."

Isaiah records the words of the Lord later in that chapter regarding, in part, the creation of this book, and in larger view the restoration of his gospel stating, "Therefore, behold, I will proceed to do a marvellous work among this people, even a marvellous work and a wonder: for the wisdom of their wise men shall perish, and the understanding of their prudent men shall be hid." The Book of Mormon is a marvelous work and a wonder. In our day, another prophecy by Ezekiel stands out because of its connection to the Book of Mormon:

> Moreover, thou son of man, take thee one stick, and write upon it, For Judah, and for the children of Israel his companions:

> then take another stick, and write upon it, For Joseph, the stick of Ephraim, and for all the house of Israel his companions: And join them one to another into one stick; and they shall become one in thine hand. Say unto them, Thus saith the Lord God; Behold, I will take the stick of Joseph, which is in the hand of Ephraim, and the tribes of Israel his fellows, and will put them with him, even with the stick of Judah, and make them one stick, and they shall be one in mine hand. And the sticks whereon thou writest shall be in thine hand before their eyes. (Ezekiel 37:16,17,19,20)

Today members of the Church of Jesus Christ of Latter-day Saints carry with them in one hand both the stick of Joseph (the Book of Mormon) and the stick of Judah (the Bible) in fulfillment of this prophecy.

38. Internal evidences and prophecies must be confirmed and fulfilled.

One of the internal prophecies proven accurate by the prophet Nephi in 2 Nephi 3:11-15 states:

> But a seer will I raise up out of the fruit of thy loins; and unto him will I give power to bring forth my word unto the

seed of thy loins—and not to the bringing forth my word only, saith the Lord, but to the convincing them of my word, which shall have already gone forth among them. Wherefore, the fruit of thy loins shall write; and the fruit of the loins of Judah shall write; and that which shall be written by the fruit of thy loins, and also that which shall be written by the fruit of the loins of Judah, shall grow together, unto the confounding of false doctrines and laying down of contentions, and establishing peace among the fruit of thy loins, and bringing them to the knowledge of their fathers in the latter days, and also to the knowledge of my covenants, saith the Lord. And out of weakness he shall be made strong, in that day when my work shall commence among all my people, unto the restoring thee, O house of Israel, saith the Lord. And thus prophesied Joseph, saying: Behold, that seer will the Lord bless; and they that seek to destroy him shall be confounded; for this promise, which I have obtained of the Lord, of the fruit of my loins, shall be fulfilled. Behold, I am sure of the fulfilling of this promise; And his name shall be called after me; and it shall be after the name of his father. And

> he shall be like unto me; for the thing, which the Lord shall bring forth by his hand, by the power of the Lord shall bring my people unto salvation.

This scripture prophesized that Joseph Smith would be a descendant of Joseph of Egypt (one of the sons of Jacob in the Bible) and that he would be a seer, blessed by the Lord. It also appears to be providing a more detailed description of the prophecy Ezekiel made in chapter thirty-seven of his book.

There were many Messianic prophecies that were fulfilled in the Book of Mormon throughout the Nephite history including the number of years until Jesus' birth (1 Ne. 10:4; Hel. 14:2), conditions surrounding his birth (1 Ne. 11:13-21), his mother's identity (Mosiah 3:8), the manner and location of his baptism by John the Baptist (1 Ne. 10:7-10), his miracles and teachings (1 Ne. 11:28-31), and his Atonement, resurrection, and second coming. Prophets foretold details concerning Christ's crucifixion and his atoning sacrifice, one stating that "blood cometh from every pore, so great shall be his anguish for the wickedness and the abominations of his people" (Mosiah 3:7). Furthermore, he would rise on the third day (2 Ne. 25:13) and appear to many (Alma 16:20). Samuel the Lamanite prophesied specific signs of Christ's birth and death that would be experienced by Book of Mormon peoples (Hel. 14). During Christ's visit to the Americas, He attested to the authenticity of these prophecies by stating that "the scriptures concerning my coming are fulfilled" (3 Ne. 9:16). Remember that every prophecy that was fulfilled was written about without looking back at the text previously written. This touches on earlier points but nonetheless is still impressive given the quantity and location of the prophecies.

39. Your book must contain several detailed descriptions of warfare. The types of warfare you describe must be unfamiliar to you.

Numerous chapters are devoted to wars in the Book of Mormon and at least fifteen major wars are described throughout the entire book. Helaman 11:25 is one small example of guerilla warfare used by the Gadianton Robbers. Guerilla warfare is common throughout the Book of Mormon and uses principles of surprise, secrecy, hidden camps, favorable terrain, small scale battles, and tactical retreats to help a smaller force overcome a larger army. It must be taken into account that Joseph had never fought in a war prior to his commencement of the translation of the Book of Mormon and therefore he had no experience from which to create such elaborate scenarios and strategies of war. Another interesting fact to consider is that warfare in Joseph's era was mainly carried out with rifles, yet warfare described in the Book of Mormon was executed using ancient weapons such as arrows, quivers, cimeters and javelins. You must likewise write about warfare styles not common in your day and not familiar to you. You must do this, having absolutely no experience in warfare.

40. You must include a system of weights and measures.

The monetary system of the Book of Mormon consisted of the following:

> Now the reckoning is thus—a senine of gold, a seon of gold, a shum of gold, and a limnah of gold. A senum of silver, an amnor of silver, an ezrom of silver, and an onti of silver. A senum of silver was equal to a senine of gold, and either for a measure of barley, and also for a measure of every kind of grain. Now the amount of a seon of gold was twice the value of a senine. And a shum of gold was twice the value of a seon. And a limnah of gold was the value of them all. And an amnor of silver was as great as two senums. And an ezrom of silver was as great as four senums. And an onti was as great as them all. Now this is the value of the lesser numbers of their reckoning— A shiblon is half of a senum; therefore, a shiblon for half a measure of barley. And a shiblum is a half of a shiblon. And a leah is the half of a shiblum. Now this is their number, according to their reckoning. Now an antion of gold is equal to three shiblons

> included a senine of gold, senum of silver.
> (Alma 11:5-19)

This system is comparable to the system of weights and measures described in the ancient Mesopotamian Laws of Eshnunna. In Eshnunna one kor of barley was priced at one shekel of silver and in like manner the Book of Mormon describes a senum of silver was equal to a senine of gold, and either for a measure of barley, as cited above. In both the Laws of Eshnunna and the Book of Mormon, precious metals and barley were exchangeable for each other. The system of weights and measures you design must also be correlated to other known civilizations of the time period in which the events in your book take place.

41. Your book must include thousands of intertextual relationships.

Intertextuality is the term used to describe the interrelationships between two or more texts. The Book of Mormon contains hundreds of connections to the Old Testament and the New Testament as well as hundreds of connections to different books within its own pages. Just have a look at the footnotes which have been added since the Book of Mormon was first published (the first edition did not contain any footnotes but the fact that they could be added at any point in time is the critical issue). While the Book of Mormon does contain several quotes from the Old Testament prophet Isaiah, and also the Psalms, there are countless other passages which correlate to biblical teachings. Only about five percent of the Book of Mormon could be considered plagiaristic yet references to the Bible are contained on almost every page.

42. Your book must include a promise that if those who read your book, pray sincerely to know the truth of its origins and content, it will be made known unto them.

In the book of Moroni, he promised the following: "And when you shall receive these things, I would exhort you that ye would ask God, the Eternal Father, in the name of Christ, if these things are not true; and if ye ask with a sincere heart, with real intent, having faith in Christ, he will manifest the truth of it unto you by the power of the Holy Ghost." (Moroni 10:4) Many people have put this invitation to the test. They have prayed about the Book of Mormon and received confirmation that it is in-fact true. In a similar way, people must be invited to know the truth of your book. Your promise must be effective in convincing millions of people to believe in your words.

43. Many of the facts, concepts, and statements presented in your book must be entirely inconsistent with the world's prevailing beliefs.

Many of the teachings brought forth in the Book

of Mormon differ from the common theological beliefs held by Christians and non-Christians in the early nineteenth century. The Book of Mormon teaches that baptism is essential for all people except for little children. The prophet Mormon had this to say regarding the subject,

> Listen to the words of Christ, your Redeemer, your Lord and your God. Behold, I came into the world not to call the righteous but sinners to repentance; the whole need no physician, but they that are sick; wherefore, little children are whole, for they are not capable of committing sin; wherefore the curse of Adam is taken from them in me, that it hath no power over them; and the law of circumcision is done away in me. And after this manner did the Holy Ghost manifest the word of God unto me; wherefore, my beloved son, I know that it is solemn mockery before God, that ye should baptize little children. Behold I say unto you that this thing shall ye teach—repentance and baptism unto those who are accountable and capable of committing sin; yea, teach parents that they must repent and be baptized, and humble themselves as their little children, and they shall all be saved with their little children. (Moroni 8:8-10)

There are still those who believe baptism isn't an essential ordinance and there are those who believe still that little children are in need of baptism.

Many people believed in the early nineteenth century and still believe today that the Bible is the only word of God, that no more scripture will be revealed. To that, the Book of Mormon prophesied, "And because my words shall hiss forth—many of the Gentiles shall say: A Bible! A Bible! We have got a Bible, and there cannot be any more Bible." (2 Nephi 29:3) The Lord continued to explain His reason for revealing more of His words when He stated the following, as Nephi records,

> Thou fool, that shall say: A Bible, we have got a Bible, and we need no more Bible. Have ye obtained a Bible save it were by the Jews? Know ye not that there are more nations than one? Know ye not that I, the Lord your God, have created all men, and that I remember those who are upon the isles of the sea; and that I rule in the heavens above and in the earth beneath; and I bring forth my word unto the children of men, yea, even upon all the nations of the earth? Wherefore murmur ye, because that ye shall receive more of my word? Know ye not that the testimony of two nations is a witness unto you that I am God, that I remember one nation like unto another? Wherefore, I speak the same words unto one nation like

> unto another. And when the two nations shall run together the testimony of the two nations shall run together also. And I do this that I may prove unto many that I am the same yesterday, today, and forever; and that I speak forth my words according to mine own pleasure. And because that I have spoken one word ye need not suppose that I cannot speak another; for my work is not yet finished; neither shall it be until the end of man, neither from that time henceforth and forever. Wherefore, because that ye have a Bible ye need not suppose that it contains all my words; neither need ye suppose that I have not caused more to be written. (2 Nephi 29:6-10)

These are just a couple examples of how the teachings and doctrines contained in the Book of Mormon greatly opposed the current beliefs of the time. There are countless other doctrines and principles it teaches that went against the common beliefs in 1830. The authority of the priesthood, the gift of the Holy Ghost and the plan of salvation are just a few more examples.

44. You must include a large, intricate parable in your book and relate it to some type of horticulture. This parable must symbolically connect to the people in your story.

In the fifth chapter of Jacob a parable is given known as the Allegory of the Olive Tree. The parable spans thousands of years from the time of Abraham to the time of the Millennium (a future event). It relates olive trees to the tribes of Israel and their history, scattering, and eventual return to their promised land in the last days. The people in the Book of Mormon are descendants of Joseph of Israel and consequently the parable applies to them. The Allegory of the Olive Tree is over 3,700 words in length. To put that in perspective, the Parable of the Sower is barely over 100 words long. How challenging would it have been to paint the thousands of years of history of the Lord's people in an extended metaphorical story?

Below are some of the symbols and their meanings from the allegory:

Symbol	Meaning
The Vineyard	The World
Tame olive tree	The house of Israel, the Lord's covenant people
Wild olive tree	Gentiles, or non-Israel (later in the parable, wild branches represent apostate Israel)
Branches	Groups of people

The roots of the tame olive tree	The gospel covenants and promises the Lord makes with His children, a constant source of strength and life to the faithful
Fruit of the tree	The lives or works of men
Digging, pruning, fertilizing	The Lord's work with His children, which seeks to persuade them to be obedient and produce good fruit
Transplanting the branches	Scattering of groups throughout the world, or restoring them to their original position
Grafting	The process of spiritual rebirth through which one is joined to the covenant
Decaying branches	Wickedness and apostasy
Casting the branches into the fire	The judgement of God

The Allegory of the Olive Tree is unique to the Book of Mormon and cannot be found anywhere else, so it was either an original story written by Zenos (as the Book of Mormon claims) or it was invented by Joseph. The fact that there was no olive culture done in New England in Joseph's day makes this an even tougher challenge for him to fabricate. How could he have known so many intricate details of olive horticulture, to then bring those details together in such a complex representation? Joseph Fielding Smith, the son of Hyrum Smith, shared his feeling regarding the remarkability of the parable, "This parable in and of itself stamps the Book of Mormon with convincing truth. No mortal man, without the inspiration of the Lord, could have written such a parable. It is a pity that too many of those who read the Book of Mormon pass over and slight the truths which it conveys in relation to the history, scattering, and final gathering of Israel" (Smith J. F., 1979).

45. Include in your book hundreds of complex, subtle, and meaningful chiasmus.

Chiasmus are literary figures in which words, sentences, grammatical constructions, or concepts are repeated in reverse order, in the same or a modified form, for ex. A, B, C, D, D, C, B, A. The entire thirty-sixth chapter of Alma is one large chiasmus; Mosiah 5 is also a chiasmus. Chiasmus can also be found throughout the Bible such as in Mark 2, Genesis 7:17, Psalm 58, and Genesis 7:21-23. We should expect the Book of Mormon to contain several since chiasmus were considered both a dominant and an essential writing style in Lehi's day. The absence of chiasmus in the Book of Mormon would certainly be deemed a deficiency. As it turns out, there are more than 350 chiasmus in the Book of Mormon, which would mean you would have to include a chiasmus on every other page of your book. The possibility that Joseph could have known about chiasmus is very remote, but even if he knew about them he still would have had the difficult task of inventing hundreds of original chiastic sentences, and in some cases entire chiastic chapters, that happen to coincide perfectly with the narration of the text.

46. Your book must include colophons.

A colophon, usually contained at the beginning or end of a text, is a publisher's emblem or imprint on his or her book. A colophon generally contains information about the addressee, author, scribe, subject material, and chronological information. The Book of Mormon contains several colophons throughout. Nephi provides a lengthy colophon at the commencement of his record. He identifies himself as the author and scribe of the text, provides a summary of his book, and then tells about his background, upraising, education, and reason for writing his book. Similarly, Enos used a colophon at the beginning of his record, Jacob used a colophon at the conclusion of his record, and Mormon used colophons throughout his entire abridgement. These examples are found in 1 Nephi 1:1, Enos 1:1-2, The Words of Mormon 1:1, and Jacob 7:27.

47. Your book must contain several original psalms of lament.

The Jews wrote psalms of lament or songs of devastation to the Lord when experiencing trials, tribulation, or suffering. Psalms of lament are found abundantly throughout the Old Testament. Roughly one-third of the psalms in the Bible contain laments. Psalms of lament typically contain the following components:

1. Invocation

2. Complaint
3. Confession of Trust
4. Petition for Help
5. Vow of Praise

There are about two dozen original psalms of lament in the Book of Mormon. Consider the profound, yet beautifully articulated psalm of lament, in 2 Nephi 4. It follows the typical components of a true psalm of lament listed above in order:

1. "Behold, my soul delighteth in the things of the Lord;" v. 16
2. "O wretched man that I am!" "I am encompassed about, because of the temptations and the sins which do so easily best me." v. 18
3. "O Lord, I have trusted in thee, and I will trust in thee forever." v. 34
4. "O Lord, wilt thou redeem my soul? Wilt thou deliver me out of the hands of mine enemies? Wilt thou make me that I may shake at the appearance of sin?" v. 31
5. "Behold, my voice shall forever ascend up unto thee, my rock and mine everlasting God." Verse 35

The Book of Mormon also references the biblical psalms about sixty times. As found in the Dead Sea Scrolls, the psalms are not always listed in the same order as the Bible but are intermixed and shuffled throughout. From what we know of the contents of the brass plates, as described in the Book of Mormon, the people of Lehi surely had a record of the psalms and referred to them often. It would have been a brilliant achievement for Joseph to have created several of his own original psalms of lament, while independently incorporating numerous biblical psalms into the narrative, and then designing a method to shuffle them precisely throughout the text in a manner that matches the storyline. If the Book of Mormon was truly written by ancient Hebrews, then it would make perfect sense for them to make frequent usage of biblical psalms in their record. It would also make sense for them to create their own original psalms of lament.

48. Your book must contain many prepositional phrases where you would typically use adverbs.

The Book of Mormon is filled with prepositional phrases because the Hebrew language does not contain as many adverbs as the English language. This would not be as challenging of a task for an author to add to his or her book. However, when we consider the differences between the Hebrew and English languages, the persistent substitution of prepositional phrases becomes an important piece in lending to the book's credibility regarding its origins. Here are some examples:

> "with patience" instead of patiently (Mosiah 24:15)

"with much harshness" instead of very harshly (1 Nephi 18:11)
"with joy" instead of joyfully (Jacob 4:3)
"in spirit and in truth" instead of spiritually and truly (Alma 34:38)
"in righteousness" instead of righteously (1 Nephi 20:1)
"with gladness" instead of gladly (2 Nephi 28:28)

49. Your book must include several examples of cognate accusatives and other Hebraisms.

A cognate accusative is a direct object noun that shares the same root as the preceding verb. Examples such as "I have dreamed a dream [Hebrew halamtî halôm]; or, in other words, I have seen a vision [hazîtî hazôn]" (1 Nephi 8:2) don't make much sense in English, but they do in Hebrew. In fact, the Hebrew Bible also contains several cognate accusatives such as "she vowed a vow" (1 Samuel 1:11), "wrote upon it a writing" (Exodus 39:30), and "the fruit tree yielding fruit" (Gen 1:11).

A Hebraism is a form of writing or speaking that uses the grammatical or rhetorical styles of Hebrew. If the Book of Mormon is just the creation of a young farm boy's imagination, how could he have thought to include so many Hebraisms, many of which are unique to the Book of Mormon? He likely didn't know what Hebraisms were when the Book of Mormon was translated, yet it contains hundreds of different examples scattered throughout its text, many of which have not even been included in this book. Examples of Hebraisms not discussed in detail in this book (though a few are alluded to) are: simple synonyms, repetitive conjunctions, gradation, if/and conditionals, repetitive resumptions, duplication, simile curses, extended alternates, typological narratives, extended synonymous, scriptural allusions, wordplays, extended synthetic, the phrase "and it came to pass", like sentence endings, like sentence beginnings, contrasting ideas, numeric conventions, poetic refrains, parallelism of numbers, parallelism of progression, random repetition, idem per idem, antithetical, enallage, epistolary form, merismus, regular repetition, repeated alternate, simple alternate, metonymy, prophetic speech, motifs and more.

50. You must create twenty-four unique, identifiable wordprints in your book.

Wordprint, or stylometry as it is more commonly known, is the forensic science used to measure an author's literary style. It can help identify the author for any text, letter, or book where the author is unknown. Each person has a unique literary fingerprint that is different from everyone else in the world. Studies have shown that through word combinations, vocabulary, punctuation, sentence structure, and frequency of word usage, each person has a personalized wordprint, much like a fingerprint, where the author can be identified.

The Book of Mormon contains twenty-four unique wordprints from twenty-four different authors. The twenty-four authors do not appear in twenty-four separate books but are shuffled and intermixed in the most complicated manner imaginable. How could anyone keep track of so many wordprints and vary each in a perfect manner when the concept of wordprint was unknown in Joseph Smith's day? Daniel Petersen, a Ph.D. in Near Eastern Languages and Cultures, stated the following,

> There is … no evidence that [Joseph] was keeping a journal or developing his writing style, no record of his writing sketches or short stories, no indication that he was creating the major characters of the Nephite history, planning its plots, or working out the major themes and ideas found in its pages; nor is there any evidence that he was consciously developing an authorial voice or cultivating a personal writing style (or that he even understood what this would have entailed). Neither did he exhibit any proclivity for composing large narrative forms or differential styles or anything at all like the complex, interwoven, episodic components of the Book of Mormon. (Rees, John Milton, Joseph Smith, and the Book of Mormon)

The complexity of the wordprint found in several books written by highly regarded nineteenth century authors such as Charles Dickens, Jane Austen, Samuel Clemens (Mark Twain) and James Fenimore Cooper, pale in comparison to the complexity of the wordprint contained in the Book of Mormon. Through the use of stylometry, the writings of Solomon Spaulding, Sidney Rigdon, and Joseph Smith have also been analyzed and found to be significantly different from the twenty-four authors of the Book of Mormon. On another occasion Daniel Peterson said, "The intricate structure and detailed complexity of the Book of Mormon seem far better explained as the work of several ancient writers using various written sources over the space of centuries than exploding suddenly from the mind of a barely educated manual laborer on the American frontier. (Petersen, 2011)

Requirements That Must Be Met After Writing Your Book

51. When you complete your book you must make no significant changes in the storyline or doctrine of the text. The only changes allowed can be grammatical, spelling, punctuation (which is later added), and typographical changes.

Critics remind us that 3,913 changes were made to the Book of Mormon after its first edition printing. The vast majority of these, however, were grammatical corrections. Although Joseph Smith was the translator of the Book of Mormon, the spelling in the first edition was Oliver Cowdery's and the punctuation was John H. Gilbert's. Other notable changes in the Book of Mormon were: Father, changed to Son of the Father; white changed to pure; and the name Benjamin changed to Mosiah. According to Daniel B. Wallace, a professor of New

Testament Studies, the Bible has undergone more than 100,000 changes.

> The original KJV had approximately 8,000 marginal notes, though these have been stripped out in modern printings of the Authorized Version. Further, some of the typos and blatant errors of the 1611 KJV have continued to remain in the text after multiple corrections and spelling updates (weighing in at more than 100,000 changes) through the 1769 edition. (Wallace, 2012)

Even though none of the original manuscripts of the Bible exist, roughly one third of the original manuscript of the Book of Mormon is still in existence. The entire printer's manuscript (which is Oliver's exact copy of the original manuscript) is also still in existence and it is freely accessible to the public at josephsmithpapers.org. The printer's manuscript was used by E. B. Grandin and John Gilbert for the typesetting of the 1830 edition of the Book of Mormon. By comparing the original 1830 edition to the printer's manuscript we can identify the errors made by those who did the typesetting. Likewise, by comparing the printer's manuscript to the current version of the Book of Mormon we can see all the changes that have been made through the years.

52. No claim or fact in your book can ever be disproved.

The Title Page of the Book of Mormon states, "And now, if there are faults they are the mistakes of men; wherefore, condemn not the things of God, that ye may be found spotless at the judgment-seat of Christ." While the Book of Mormon may have contained several grammatical or typographical mistakes, none of the facts or claims within its pages have ever been disproven. Many theories and opinions have been provided over the years by critics of the Book of Mormon, regarding its theological, scientific, or historical contents, yet each time an argument is presented against it, more research is given to that specific subject and eventually evidence in support of that subject arises. All claims against the Book of Mormon have proven beneficial for further research, discovery, and subsequent validation of the veracity of its contents.

53. Your book cannot contain any *proven* anachronisms. Every custom, event or object must fit precisely within the correct historical and chronological timeframe.

Critics often point out that the Book of Mormon's mentions of chariots, horses, elephants, swords etc. were all out of place and time. However, the more we discover, the more we realize they weren't. In fact, horse and elephant bones and swords have all been discovered, pointing to the historical accuracy of the Book of Mormon. There can be argument made on both sides, but what used to be thought of as an anachronism can become a relevant historical fact with one archeological discovery. For example, in Joseph's day many people criticized him for claiming that the record from which he translated the Book of Mormon into English was written on gold plates. This was thought of as preposterous; everyone knew that the ancients wrote on papyrus. However, in 1933 a German archeologist by the name of Friedrich Krefter discovered the plates of King Darius I, also known as "Darius the Great" of Persia. They were written on both silver and gold plates and estimated to have been inscribed around 513 B.C. According to the Book of Mormon, Nephi first began to inscribe on the gold plates around 580 B.C. Interestingly, the King Darius plates were also stored in a cement box, in the same manner the Book of Mormon plates were stored. Even the famous fiction writer J.K. Rowling has admitted to including anachronisms in her books. In her book titled "Fantastic Beasts and Where to Find Them" she tells of a debate that took place in Washington in the year 1777. However, as pointed out by Radio Times, Washington wasn't actually founded until 1790, thirteen years after the event took place. Mistakes can be made even when writing fictitious stories. Anachronisms are tough to debate because we are still discovering historical artifacts almost daily. Another example of this is the claim that millions of people couldn't have existed in the Book of Mormon lands (if the events occurred in central or Mesoamerica as many believe) and therefore there could not have been hundreds of thousands of deaths in the final battle of the Nephites at Cumorah, as reported by Mormon. A new technology called LiDAR (Light Detection and Ranging) has helped uncover more than 60,000 hidden Mayan structures in Guatemala suggesting the population was between 10-15 million during 250 A.D., when it was previously believed that the population could only have been five million at most. History can change in an instant. That is why the key for this point is that your book must not contain any *proven* anachronisms.

54. Archaeological discovery and scientific evidence for the next 185 years must verify the claims in your book.

Archaeological evidence and satellite discoveries have led to the validation of many potential sites for the Book of Mormon events. The following are only a few of the many evidences that have been discovered over the years.

There are several place names in the Book of Mormon that can be correlated to modern locations today such as Tabasco, Jershon, Lamania and Nahom.

> The city of Lamanai (from Lama'anayin, 'submerged crocodile' in Yucatec Maya) is a Mesoamerican archaeological site and was once a major city of the Maya civilization, located in the north of Belize, in Orange Walk District. The site's name is pre-Columbian, recorded by early Spanish missionaries, and was documented over a

> millennium earlier in Mayan inscriptions as Lam'an'ain (Wikipedia, n.d.).

The fact that this city was Mayan (which coincides with the time-frame of the Nephites), and that it kept its original name, is significant: this city could very well be the city of Lamoni, a Lamanite king. Mesoamerica has long been thought to be the land of the Book of Mormon events, and this area in Belize coincides with current scholar's beliefs of where the Lamanite lands were really located. In fact, the current map of V. Garth Norman, titled "Mesoamerica and Book of Mormon Lands," suggests that the area where Lamanai is located was Lamanite territory at the time of the Lamanite King Lamoni (around 90 B.C.).

Across the ocean and from an earlier time in the Book of Mormon, three altar inscriptions have been found at the Bar'an Temple located in Marib—about seventy miles east of San'a, Yemen—which contain the inscription NHM. There is a strong correlation between NHM and the place called Nahom in the Book of Mormon, because in Hebrew Nahom would have been spelled NHM. In 1 Nephi 16:34 it states the following, "And it came to pass that Ishmael died, and was buried in the place which was called Nahom." The word NHM in Hebrew relates to sorrow, consoling and mourning. This meaning is very appropriate, given Nephi's description of Nahom as the place where they buried Ishmael, whom they undoubtedly mourned.

In the first verse of the following chapter it states,

"And it came to pass that we did again take our journey in the wilderness; and we did travel nearly eastward from that time forth." If you travel nearly eastward from where these altars are located, you will eventually hit the coast of the Wadi Sayq, which contains lush vegetation, fresh water, iron ore, honey and suitable conditions for the land Bountiful as described in the Book of Mormon. Many discoveries have been made that support the location of Nephi's Bountiful in modern day Khor Kharfot, Oman, and the location of (NHM) Nahom matches perfectly with the description provided in the Book of Mormon and the geography of the area.

The following requirements must all exist in one location in order to be considered Bountiful:

The location must lie nearly eastward of Nahom (1 Nephi 17:1)
The coast must be accessible from the interior desert.
Both the general area and the location when the Lehites camped must be fertile and capable of producing crops.
It must be a coastal location (1 Nephi 17:5).
It must be very fertile, with "much fruit and also wild honey" and small game (1 Nephi 17:5-6).
Timber must be available with which to build a ship (1 Nephi 17:8).
Freshwater must be available year-round.
A mountain must be located nearby to account for Nephi's reference to going to a mountain to "pray oft" (1 Nephi 18:3).

Cliffs overlooking the ocean must be present to account for Nephi's brother's attempt to throw him "into the depths of the sea" (1 Nephi 17:48).
Ore and flint must be available with which to make fire and fabricate tools to build a ship" (1 Nephi 17:9)
No resident population can be present at the time of the Lehites' arrival.
Wind and ocean currents capable of carrying a ship out into the ocean must be present (1 Nephi 18:8).

Here's what we find when examining the area of the Wadi Sayq and Khor Kharfot, Oman:

Khor Kharfot is situated less than one degree from due east of Nehem (Nahom).
The valley of Wadi Sayq leads to the ocean from the desert interior and is the only wadi that flows from the high desert eastward toward the coast; the coast is accessible by traveling through the bottom of Wadi Sayq.
Khor Kharfot is the most fertile site on the southern Arabian coast; the region of fertility extends two miles into the Wadi Sayq.
There is evidence of inhabitation and use as a small seaport during the Islamic period.
A number of good-sized trees exist in the area, with evidence of ancient forests. These trees could have provided plenty of lumber to build a ship.
Khor Kharfot has the largest permanent flow of fresh water of any site on the coast, available through freshwater springs and an ancient river.
A large mountain overlooks the west end of the beach.

Cliffs rise above the ocean in this area.
Iron in the form of specular hematite is available in the Marbat plain, within a few days' hike to the east of Khor Kharfot.
A form of flint is available on the surface in large quantities.
Ancient ruins show that Khor Kharfot was occupied intermittently, although it is currently uninhabited.
The coast is well suited for sailing, with seasonal winds in the fall blowing east.

Although no indication has been provided by the general authorities of the Church of Jesus Christ of Latter-day Saints that Khor Kharfot is the actual location of Lehi's Bountiful, it seems very likely given the mountain of evidence that agrees with the text of the Book of Mormon.

Another possible parallel can be found in Mesoamerican theology. Quetzalcoatl is a deity who is often related to Jesus Christ. Quetzalcoatl was said to have helped create mankind, was born of a virgin mother, was associated with the bread of life, shed his blood to save mankind, was considered the deity of resurrection, was responsible for the rebirth of the deceased, and was considered a personage of light associated with the sun. More than 1,300 years had passed since Christ's visit to the ancient Americas, according to the Book of Mormon, and that amount of time would have allowed many erroneous teachings to have distorted the original stories and traditions which were repeated down through the centuries. While we don't know for sure whether Quetzalcoatl was in-fact

Jesus Christ, the many similarities concerning the two deities are difficult to simply write off.

The Book of Mormon also mentions highways or roads in the following books and verses: Helaman 7:10, 14:24, and 3 Nephi 6:8, 8:13. This was considered an anachronism at the time, because none of the ancient American cultures supposedly had roads. Recently, however, over 100 miles of roads or highways have been discovered in Guatemala alone. As modern technology advances and as more effort is given, more evidences may be revealed. What we know about history today may be changed completely by one archeological find tomorrow.

55. You must invite the world's brightest scholars, historians, scientists, experts, and all who wish to prove your book a forgery by exposing even the tiniest mistake, to carefully examine it.

The Book of Mormon has been around for nearly two centuries and has been reviewed, analyzed, and scrutinized by millions of people. "This complex book [the Book of Mormon] has been read and scrutinized in many ways: textually, doctrinally, historically, comparatively, literarily, legally, statistically, geographically, philosophically, practically, biographically, intellectually, prayerfully, and spiritually—to name some of the most obvious" (Welch, The Miraculous Timing of the Translation of the Book of Mormon, 2017), and in the words of Jeffrey R. Holland, a modern-day apostle of the Lord,

> For 179 years this book has been examined and attacked, denied and deconstructed, targeted and torn apart like perhaps no other book in modern religious history – perhaps like no other book in *any* religious history. And still it stands. Failed theories about its origins have been born and parroted and have died – from Ethan Smith to Solomon Spaulding to deranged paranoid to cunning genius. None of these frankly pathetic answers for this book has ever withstood examination because *there is no other answer* than the one Joseph gave as its young unlearned translator. In this I stand with my own great-grandfather, who said simply enough, 'No wicked man could write such a book as this; and no good man would write it, unless it were true and he were commanded of God to do so.' (Holland, 2009)

56. Tens of thousands of intellectual men and women, scholars, researchers, and professionals must believe in and follow the teachings of your book.

It is a mistake to assume that anyone who believes in the Book of Mormon is either uneducated, ignorant, or deceived. Millions of women and men around the world, from all different cultures, backgrounds, ethnicities, traditions, and with a variety of educational backgrounds have thoroughly studied the Book of Mormon and believe in its teachings. When gathered collectively, they make up a body of believers as diverse as any in the world. Countless believers with different degrees in almost every profession exist in the world today. Many are highly educated and respected individuals in their communities. Your book must likewise be received and believed by tens of thousands of the world's most educated men and women.

57. Physical copies of your book must be published in nearly every nation and language worldwide in less than 200 years.

In the April, 2011 General Conference of the Church of Jesus Christ of Latter-day Saints, it was mentioned that more than 150 million copies had been published in eight-five different languages. Not only would it be a difficult task to write a book and publish it in almost every nation in less than 200 years, it would be a major achievement to still have your book in print 200 years after you write the first edition. How many other books written in 1829 are still in print today? If you are going to write a book comparable to the Book of Mormon, it must be of equal popularity. The Book of Mormon is still one of the most popular books ever written.

58. You must affirm that your story is not fiction.

It would be much less challenging to write a work of fiction than it would be to claim that your book is based on real events. If your book is based on real events, then it must line up with other known events in history from the same era. On the flip side, even the most minute or insignificant pieces of history that don't seem to match your story will be used to lambaste your legacy. Famous works of fiction such as J.R.R Tolkien's *The Lord of the Rings* should not be compared to the Book of Mormon. While these books combined perhaps compare to the Book of Mormon in complexity, it should be taken into account that it took the internationally renowned Oxford English professor twelve years to write the first edition, and as any work of fiction, it cannot be related to any real events, names, or places in history. Many of the greatest works of fiction often compared to the Book of Mormon were written by authors who had significantly more time and education than Joseph. It would have been much simpler for Joseph to pawn off the Book of Mormon as a work of fiction rather than claim it is an ancient historical record. If it is a work of fiction, then there shouldn't be one ounce of evidence to support it. However, in this book there are several evidences mentioned that support the Book of Mormon as an ancient historical record.

***In addition to the many requirements already listed, points 59-62 are of a spiritual nature and may prove impossible to perform. However, they should be remembered and considered nonetheless, as a part of the overall challenge to write a book comparable to the Book of Mormon.**

59. Three credible witnesses must testify to the world that an angel from heaven appeared to them and confirmed the truthfulness of your book.

Many people heard Martin Harris testify of what he had seen and heard as one of the Three Witnesses. One person reported him saying, "It is not a mere belief, but is a matter of knowledge. I saw the plates and the inscriptions thereon. I saw the angel, and he showed them unto me" (Anderson R. L., 1989). David Whitmer was even asked once if he had been mistaken and had been under some hallucination which perhaps had deceived him and the other witnesses into thinking they saw an angel show him the plates. His response was "No, sir! I was not under any hallucination, nor was I deceived! I saw with these eyes and I heard with these ears! I know whereof I speak!" (Cook, David Whitmer Interviews, 1991). He died in 1875, solid in his testimony of the Book of Mormon and the gospel of Jesus Christ. When Martin Harris was asked if he was sure he saw the angel and the records of the Book of Mormon in the form of gold plates he replied, "Gentlemen," and he held out his right hand, "do you see that hand? Are you sure you see it? Are your eyes playing a trick or something? No. Well as sure as you see my hand so sure did I see the angel and the plates. Brethren, I know I saw and heard these things, and the Lord knows I know these things of which I have spoken are true" (Anderson R. L., 1981). Oliver Cowdery told Jacob Gates in the year 1849, "Jacob, I want you to remember what I say to you. I am a dying man, and what would it profit me to tell you a lie? I know," said he, "that this Book of Mormon was translated by the gift and power of God. My eyes saw, my ears heard, and my understanding was touched, and I know that whereof I testified is true. It was no dream, no vain imagination of the mind-it was real." (Gates, 1912)

60. The voice of the Redeemer must proclaim from heaven, His approval of your book. He must declare to each of the three witnesses that your book is true.

In the Testimony of the Three Witnesses in the Book of Mormon it states, "Be it known unto all nations, kindreds, tongues, and people, unto whom this work shall come: That we, through the grace of God the Father, and our Lord Jesus Christ, have seen the plates which contain this record, which is a record of the people of Nephi, and also of the Lamanites, their brethren, and also of the people of Jared, who came from the tower of which hath been spoken. And we also know that they have been translated by the gift and power of God, for his voice hath declared it unto us; wherefore we know of a surety that the work is true." Each of the three witnesses heard the voice of the Lord confirm that the Book of Mormon had been translated by the gift and power of God. This was the ultimate affirmation that the book they had observed was truly divine.

61. Eight other credible witnesses must testify to the world your book is of heavenly origin and that it was made manifest to them by divine means.

In the Spring of 1832, Samuel H. Smith told a group of people that he was a witness of the Book of Mormon. "He knew his brother Joseph had the plates, for the Prophet had shown them to him, and he had handled them and seen the engravings thereon" (Tyler, 1883). Joseph Fielding wrote,

> I visited Kirtland, the place where the Saints were, and conversed with brother Joseph Smith, and with his father and mother, and with many of the Saints. Martin Harris, one of the Three Witnesses of the Book of Mormon, gave me a particular description of the plates and of the Urim and Thummim, etc. My sister [the wife of Hyrum Smith] bears testimony that her husband has seen and handled the plates, etc.; in short I see no reason that anyone can have for rejecting this work. (Pratt, 1841)

John Whitmer said,

> I desire to testify to all . . . that I have most assuredly seen the plates from whence the Book of Mormon is translated, and that I have handled these plates and know of a surety that Joseph Smith, Jr., has

> translated the Book of Mormon by the gift and power of God, and in this thing the wisdom of the wise most assuredly has perished. (Whitmer, 1836)

When John Whitmer was asked, "Did you see [the plates] covered with a cloth?" he answered emphatically, "No. [Joseph Smith] handed them uncovered into our hands, and we turned the leaves sufficient to satisfy us" (Poulson, 1878). Each of the eight witnesses received a personal witness of the truthfulness of the Book of Mormon. While their testimonies came in the form of viewing the actual metal records, witnesses to your book must have some other type of evidence shown them that confirms your book as being of heavenly origin.

62. Each of these eleven combined witnesses must bear their testimonies to the world not for money or bribe, but under great personal sacrifices, severe persecution, even to their death beds.

Despite the fact that most of the eleven witnesses eventually had serious differences with Joseph Smith, or even left the Church, none ever denied the truthfulness of the Book of Mormon and its divine origins. None of the eleven witnesses were ever bribed or given money for their testimonies. On the contrary, they were persecuted and reviled for most of their lives. Their testimonies came at great personal cost that each was willing to bear freely for as long as he lived. The final statements of several of the witnesses have been recorded while on their deathbeds, verifying that even then, they asserted the truthfulness of the Book of Mormon. Your witnesses must be willing to do the equivalent.

63. You must find someone to finance your book, knowing that neither you nor he will ever receive any monetary remuneration for it.

The money for the first edition of the Book of Mormon was funded by Martin Harris. He paid $3,000 for 5,000 copies. "Three thousand dollars is a generous loan in any era. That amount in 1830 would be equal to $67,000 today. By some estimates, however, if you compare Martin's wealth to the local economy at that time, his gift would be worth more than $1.6 million today" (LDS, 2007). Martin was granted permission to sell the Book of Mormon in order to repay the debt he incurred from mortgaging his house and farm but the book did not sell very well. The original price of the book was $1.25 per copy. He eventually sold his 151 acres of land to repay the debt. You must find such a generous donor, willing to sacrifice an equivalent amount of land and/or money, to help you publish your book.

64. For the rest of your life you must witness the persecution, agony, starvation, and murder of those that adhere to the teachings in your book, including your dearest family and friends.

Everyone associated with Joseph Smith and the Church of Jesus Christ of Latter-day Saints would potentially subject themselves to scrutiny, persecution, violence, and in some cases death. It is no secret that Latter-day Saints by the thousands were frequently attacked and forced out of their homes and communities in the mid-nineteenth century. Many eventually made the trek out west where they would suffer countless more afflictions. One example of the cruelty that early church members were subject to was known as the Haun's Mill Massacre. Haun's Mill Massacre was a direct attack on members of the Church of Jesus Christ of Latter-day Saints who had settled in Caldwell County, Missouri in 1838. An unauthorized militia shot and killed seventeen men and boys, and injured another fifteen men, women, and children. When Joseph heard of this news, he was devastated. Imagine a religious movement being generated because of your book, then receiving the news that many people were being forced out of their homes, brutalized, and executed because of it. Would you then still hold to your claim that your book is divine?

65. You must be willing to forfeit a normal, peaceful life, risk tarnishing your family name for generations to come, suffer severe persecution the rest of your life and ultimately sacrifice your life for the sake of your book, leaving your wife husbandless and your children fatherless.

Joseph told the twelve apostles, his wife Emma, and

others the following before being taken to the Carthage jail, just prior to his death, "I am going like a lamb to the slaughter; but I am calm as a summer's morning; I have a conscience void of offense towards God, and towards all men. I shall die innocent, and it shall yet be said of me—he was murdered in cold blood" (Doctrine and Covenants Section 135:4). Joseph left behind his 39-year-old wife and five young children. Imagine how hard it would be to know you're going to die for your beliefs, and ponder on the young children and wife you will leave behind as a sacrifice for what you believe to be true. Joseph had many opportunities to renounce all that he had said and done, yet he never did. His testimony, and that of his brother Hyrum's, were sealed with their own blood. This is the concluding test that you must be willing to complete in order to write a book comparable to the Book of Mormon.

Conclusion

I sincerely believe that if anyone had the ability to write a book comparable to the Book of Mormon that they would have already done it, as proof that Joseph Smith was a charlatan. Yet here we are, nearly 200 years later, and no one has been able to write anything even close to an equivalent. It is easy to judge a book by its cover. It is easy to say that Joseph was a fraud and that the Book of Mormon is a scam. But the more carefully one examines the Book of Mormon, the more one can begin to see the marvel that it really is. This book has presented many of the facts related to the Book of Mormon and the process by which it came about. It helps clarify the difficulties and impossible nature of simply writing such a book. By doing so, it helps shed light on the true character of the book's translator. Joseph was a good man, respectable in his community, hardworking, honest, and charitable. He could not have written the Book of Mormon, and would not have done so, unless commanded by God.

Elder Jeffrey R. Holland, a modern-day apostle of Jesus Christ shared one of the most powerful testimonies of the Book of Mormon that I've heard to this day,"

When Joseph Smith and his brother Hyrum started for Carthage to face what they knew would be an imminent martyrdom, Hyrum read these words to comfort the heart of his brother:

'Thou hast been faithful; wherefore … thou shalt be made strong, even unto the sitting down in the place which I have prepared in the mansions of my Father.'

Later, when actually incarcerated in the jail, Joseph the Prophet turned to the guards who held him captive and bore a powerful testimony of the divine authenticity of the Book of Mormon. Shortly thereafter pistol and ball would take the lives of these two testators.

In this their greatest—and last—hour of need, I ask you: would these men blaspheme before God by continuing to fix their lives, their honor, and their own search for eternal salvation on a book (and by implication a church and a ministry) they had fictitiously created out of whole cloth? Never mind that their wives are about to be widows and their children fatherless. Never mind that their little band of followers will yet be 'houseless,

> friendless and homeless' and that their children will leave footprints of blood across frozen rivers and an untamed prairie floor. Never mind that legions will die and other legions live declaring in the four quarters of this earth that they know the Book of Mormon and the Church which espouses it to be true. Disregard all of that, and tell me whether in this hour of death these two men would enter the presence of their Eternal Judge quoting from and finding solace in a book which, if not the very word of God, would brand them as imposters and charlatans until the end of time? They would not do that! They were willing to die rather than deny the divine origin and the eternal truthfulness of the Book of Mormon. (Holland, 2009)

One of my favorite quotes in the Bible is from 1 Corinthians 1:27, where it states, "*But God hath chosen the foolish things of the world to confound the wise; and God hath chosen the weak things of the world to confound the things which are mighty.*" Joseph was certainly one of the weak things of the world. He was as simple as they come. He grew up on a farm and was not very well educated; like the fishermen that Jesus selected along the way, he was hardworking and unlearned. Many consider him, his translation, and his method of translating foolish. Nevertheless, he was chosen by God to translate the Book of Mormon, a task and a book that have stood the test of time. Of this, I have no doubt.

Acknowledgements

I have to start by thanking my beautiful wife, Marisol Baker, for her tremendous patience, love, and sacrifice while I worked on this book. Thank you for all the days and nights helping to take care of the kids and performing household duties while you allowed me to write. I love you so much and want you to know that I couldn't have done this without your incredible love and support.

I would like to thank my mother, Debra, for the countless hours of review, editing, and efforts on the works cited. I would also like to thank her for the many ideas and suggestions she gave me for this book. As always Mom, you've shown tremendous support for everything good I've strived to do in my life. It has been fun to partner with you in this work. I know that many generations in our family will be blessed because of your contributions.

A special thanks to my good friend, and brother in Christ, Matthew Bielert for the numerous hours he spent with me, brainstorming ideas for this book. I give personal credit to you for several ideas contained herein.

Thank you April Oguey for taking the photograph for the back cover of this book.

I would like to thank Scott Darrington for carefully reviewing and editing this book.

I'd also like to thank Hugh Nibley, John Welch, Daniel Peterson, Randal A. Wright, and all those involved in any of the publications and references listed in the works cited of this book for their years of research and hard work in helping to further our knowledge and understanding of the Book of Mormon.

Works Cited

Anderson, R. L. (1989). Investigating the Book of Mormon Witnesses. Salt Lake City: Deseret Book.

Black, S., & Wilcox, B. (2011). 188 Unexplainable Names: Book of Mormon Names No Fiction Writer Would Choose. Religious Educator, 12(2), 119-133.

Briggs, E. C. (1884, June 21). Interview with David Whitmer. The Saints' Herald, p. 396.

Cook, L. W. (1991). David Whitmer Interviews. (L. W. Cook, Ed.) Orem: Grandin Book Company.

Cook, L. W. (1991). David Whitmer Interviews. Orem: Grandin Book Company.

Cook, L. W. (1991). David Whitmer Interviews: A Restoration Witness. Orem: Grandin Book Company.

Daniels, M. (1980). The Ingenious Pen: American Writing Implements from the Eighteenth Century to to Twentieth. The American Archivist, 312-324.

Easton, S. W. (1978, July). Names of Christ in the Book of Mormon. Ensign.

Gates, J. (1912, March). Testimony of Jacob Gates. Improvement Era, pp. 418-19.

Holland, J. R. (2009, October). The Church of Jesus Christ of Latter-day Saints General Conference. Retrieved from lds.org website: https://www.lds.org/general-conference/2009/10/safety-for-the-soul?lang=eng

LDS, P. (2007, March 28). Church History: Martin Harris' Wallet is Donated to LDS Church. Retrieved from LDS Philanthropies Web site: https://www.ldsphilanthropies.org/church-history/news-features/martin-harris-wallet

Letterbook 1, p. 1. (2017, November 10). Retrieved November 10, 2017, from josephsmithpapers.org: http://www.josephsmithpapers.org

Ludlow, D. H. (1992). Encyclopedia of Mormonism (Vol. I). (D. H. Ludlow, Ed.) New York: Macmillan Publishing Company.

Mormon. (2013). The Book of Mormon Another Testament of Jesus Christ. Salt Lake City: The Church of Jesus Christ of Latter-day Saints.

Nibley, H. (1989). Literary Style in the Book of Mormon Ensured Accurate Translation. In H. Nibley, The Prophetic Book of Mormon (The Collected Works of Hugh Nibley) (Vol. 8, pp. 214-218). Salt Lake City: Deseret Book.

Peterson, D. (2011, October 27). Defending the Faith: Book of Mormon's consistency, complexity still amaze. Deseret News. Salt Lake City, Utah: Deseret News.

Poulson, P. W. (1878, August 14). Correspondence: Death of John Whitmer. Deseret News, p. 2.

Pratt, P. P. (Ed.). (1841, August). Letter from Joseph Fielding. The Latter-day Saints' Millennial Star, 2(4), pp. 52-53.

Rees, R. A. (2015). John Milton, Joseph Smith, and the Book of Mormon. BYU Studies Quarterly, 54(3), 6-18.

Rees, R. A. (2016). Joseph Smith, the Book of Mormon, and the American Renaissance: An Update. Interpreter: A Journal of Mormon Scripture, 19, 11.

Reynolds, N. B. (1997, May 27). Retrieved February 13, 2018, from BYU Speeches Web site: https://speeches.byu.edu/talks/noel-b-reynolds_authorship-book-mormon/

Skinner, E. P. (1906, October 7). Photograph album presented to President Joseph F. Smith by Junius Wells.

Sloan, D. E. (1997). The Book of Lehi and the Plates of Lehi. Journal of Book of Mormon Studies, 6(2), 269-72.

Smith, J. (2013). Pearl of Great Price, Joseph Smith History, 1:64. Salt Lake City: Church of Jesus Christ of Latter-day Saints.

Smith, J. F. (1979). Answers to Gospel Questions (Vol. 4). Salt Lake City: Deseret Book Company.

Smith, J. I. (1879, October 1). Last Testimony of Sister Emma. The Saint's Herald, 26, pp. 289-290.

Smith, J., & Jessee, D. C. (2002). The Personal Writings of Joseph Smith. (D. C. Jessee, Ed.) Salt Lake City: Deseret Book Co.

Smith, L. M. (2017, October 26). Lucy Mack Smith, History, 1845. Retrieved October 26, 2017, from josephsmithpapers.org: http://www.josephsmithpapers.org

The Doctrine and Covenants of the Church of Jesus Christ of Latter-day Saints. (2013). Salt Lake City: The Church of Jesus Christ Of Latter-day Saints.

Toone, T. (2017, November 11). BYU professor's lecture examines the timeline of Joseph Smith's translation of the Book of Mormon. Deseret News.

Tyler, D. (1883). Scraps of Biography. Juvenile Instructor Office, p. 23.

Vogel, D. (2004). Joseph Smith, The Making of a Prophet. Salt Lake City: Signature Books.

Wallace, D. B. (2012, October 8). Daniel B. Wallace. Retrieved from danielbwallace.com: https://danielbwallace.com/2012/10/08/fifteen-myths-about-bible-translation

Welch, J. W. (2017, January 25). The Miraculous Timing of the Translation of the Book of Mormon. BYU Studies.

Welch, J. W., & Rathbone, T. (1986). The Translation of the Book of Mormon: Basic Historical Information. Provo: F.A.R.M.S. Paper.

Whitmer, J. (1836, March). Kirtland, Ohio, March 1836 Address. Messenger and Advocate, 2(6), pp. 286-87.

Wikipedia, t. f. (n.d.). Lamanai. Retrieved November 30, 2017, from Wikipedia Web site: https://en.wikipedia.org/wiki/Lamanai

Printed in the United States
By Bookmasters